SPRING WEATHER

by J. P. Press

Consultant: Beth Gambro
Reading Specialist, Yorkville, Illinois

BEARPORT
PUBLISHING

Minneapolis, Minnesota

Teaching Tips

Before Reading

- Look at the cover of the book. Discuss the picture and the title.

- Ask readers to brainstorm a list of what they already know about spring weather. What can they expect to see in the book?

- Go on a picture walk, looking through the pictures to discuss vocabulary and make predictions about the text.

During Reading

- Read for purpose. Encourage readers to think about the weather they might see in the spring as they are reading.

- Ask readers to look for the details of the book. What kinds of weather are included?

- If readers encounter an unknown word, ask them to look at the sounds in the word. Then, ask them to look at the rest of the page. Are there any clues to help them understand?

After Reading

- Encourage readers to pick a buddy and reread the book together.

- Ask readers to name three types of weather from the book that can happen during spring. Go back and find the pages that tell about each type.

- Ask readers to write or draw something they learned about spring weather.

Credits:

Cover and title page, © Ирина Мещерякова/iStock; 3, © Fotyma/Shutterstock, © Korneevskiy/Shutterstock; 5, © Sv Svetlana/Shutterstock; 6, © Ruslan Kudrin/Shutterstock, © Denisfilm/iStock; 7, © emholk/iStock; 8–9, © Umomos/Shutterstock; 10–11, © monkeybusinessimages/iStock; 13, © LightField Studios/Shutterstock; 14–15, © torwai/iStock; 17, © Serenko Natalia/Shutterstock; 18–19, © John D Sirlin/Shutterstock; 20–21, © Rawpixel.com/Shutterstock; 22, © VectorMine/Shutterstock; 23TL, © Kativ/iStock; 23TM, © Lopolo/Shutterstock; 23TR, © SJ Travel Photo and Video/Shutterstock; 23BL, © Ajdin Kamber/Shutterstock; 23BM, © kozorog/iStock; 23BR, © Maxiphoto/iStock.

Library of Congress Cataloging-in-Publication Data

Names: Press, J. P., 1993- author.
Title: Spring weather / by J.P. Press ; consultant, Beth Gambro, Reading
   Specialist, Yorkville, Illinois.
Description: Bearcub books. | Minneapolis, Minnesota : Bearport Publishing
   Company, [2022] | Series: Seasons of fun: spring | Includes
   bibliographical references and index.
Identifiers: LCCN 2021030923 (print) | LCCN 2021030924 (ebook) | ISBN
   9781636913988 (library binding) | ISBN 9781636914039 (paperback) | ISBN
   9781636914084 (ebook)
Subjects: LCSH: Spring--Juvenile literature. | Weather--Juvenile
   literature.
Classification: LCC QB637.5 .P74 2022 (print) | LCC QB637.5 (ebook) |
   DDC 508.2--dc23
LC record available at https://lccn.loc.gov/2021030923
LC ebook record available at https://lccn.loc.gov/2021030924

For more information, write to Bearport Publishing, 5357 Penn Avenue South, Minneapolis, MN 55419. Printed in the United States of America.

Contents

A Season of Change

It is time for spring fun!

Spring weather brings lots of **changes**.

What will the weather be like today?

Weather in winter
can be cold.

As spring comes,
it warms up.

We put away
our mittens.

It is time to
get our shorts!

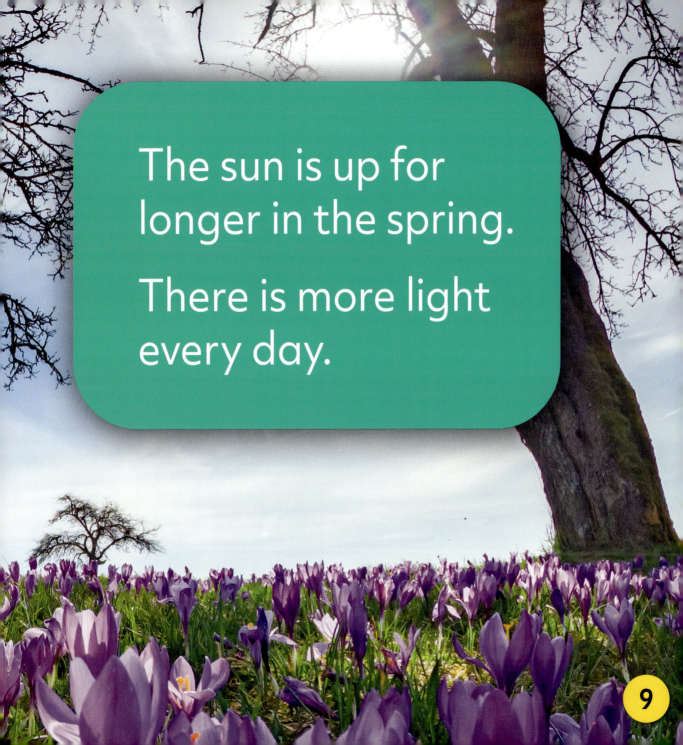

The sun is up for longer in the spring.

There is more light every day.

9

Some days in spring are still cold.

But other days are good for playing outside.

Today it is sunny.

Let's go **enjoy** the weather!

Soon, the wind starts to blow.

It brings in cold air.

Weather can change fast in the spring.

Gray clouds fill the sky.

It starts to rain.

Drip, drip, drop!

Let's put on our raincoats.

Rain boots keep our feet dry.

My brother loves to play in **puddles**.

It is so much fun to splash and **stomp**.

Then, it starts to rain harder.

We go inside when we hear **thunder**.

Boom!

Spring rain can turn into storms.

The sun will be out again soon.

There are plenty of warm days ahead.

We love spring weather!

All about Spring Rains

1 Rain starts as water on the ground. It can come from **melting** snow. It comes from rivers and lakes, too.

2 The water floats to the sky in tiny drops that we cannot see. The drops come together into clouds.

3 When clouds have too much water, the water falls as rain!

Glossary

changes the act of becoming different

enjoy to have fun or be happy with something

melting turning from solid to liquid

puddles small pools of water on the ground

stomp to step very hard

thunder a loud sound that comes from storms

Index

Read More

Brundle, Harriet. *Rain (Weather Explorers).* New York: Enslow Publishing, 2020.

Murray, Julie. *Spring Weather (Seasons: Spring Cheer!).* Minneapolis: Abdo Publishing, 2021.

Learn More Online

1. Go to **www.factsurfer.com** or scan the QR code below.
2. Enter "**Spring Weather**" into the search box.
3. Click on the cover of this book to see a list of websites.

About the Author

J. P. Press likes reading books and being outside. She loves the first warm days of spring weather.